Sermons For Pentecost II Based On First Lesson Texts For Cycle C

Lord, Send The Wind

James McLemore

CSS Publishing Company, Inc., Lima, Ohio

SERMONS FOR PENTECOST II BASED ON FIRST LESSON TEXTS
FOR CYCLE C: LORD, SEND THE WIND

Copyright © 1997 by
CSS Publishing Company, Inc.
Lima, Ohio

Some scripture quotations are from the *Holy Bible, New International Version.* Copyright © 1973, 1978, 1984 International Bible Society. Used by permission of Zondervan Bible Publishers. All rights reserved.

Some scripture quotations are from the *Revised Standard Version of the Bible,* copyrighted 1946, 1952 ©, 1971, 1973, by the Division of Christian Education of the National Council of the Churches of Christ in the USA. Used by permission.

Library of Congress Cataloging-in-Publication Data

McLemore, James H., 1946-
    Sermons for Pentecost II based on first lesson texts for cycle C : Lord, send the wind
/ James H. McLemore.
        p.   cm.
    ISBN 0-7880-1039-5 (pbk.)
    1. Pentecost season — Sermons. 2. Bible. O.T. — Sermons. 3. Sermons, American.
I. Title. II. Title: Sermons for Pentecost 2 based on first lesson texts for cycle C.   III.
Title: Sermons for Pentecost two based on first lesson texts for cycle C.   IV. Title: Maybe
your God is too small.
BV4300.5.M35   1997
252'.64—DC21
                                                                                        96-46506
                                                                                            CIP

This book is available in the following formats, listed by ISBN:
    0-7880-1039-5   Book
    0-7880-1086-7   Mac
    0-7880-1087-5   IBM 3 1/2
    0-7880-1088-3   Sermon Prep

PRINTED IN U.S.A.

To my wife,
Donna

Editor's Note Regarding The Lectionary

During the past two decades there has been an attempt to move in the direction of a uniform lectionary among various Protestant denominations.

Preaching on the same scripture lessons every Sunday is a step in the right direction of uniting Christians of many faiths. If we are reading the same scriptures together, we may also begin to accomplish other achievements. Our efforts will be strengthened through our unity.

Beginning with Advent 1995 The Evangelical Lutheran Church in America dropped its own lectionary schedule and adopted the Revised Common Lectionary.

Reflecting this change, resources published by CSS Publishing Company put their major emphasis on the Revised Common Lectionary texts for the church year.

Table Of Contents

Preface

Economic and social disparity and moral and religious corruption were the core issues of a disintegrating society in the days of Amos, Hosea, Isaiah, and Jeremiah. Each of these men received a God-given assignment. Their assignment was to create an awareness among the people of their nation that the social problems and economic ills that were plaguing their society were a direct result of a rift in their relationship with God. And to repair this rift they would have to change their attitude toward God and their relationship with each other.

Today, 2,700 years later, our society is plagued by problems similar to those witnessed by these ancient prophets. Like the society addressed by Amos, we are a society which is unfair in our treatment of persons of different races and different classes. Like the family of Hosea, we are unstable in our relationships between husbands and wives. Like the covenant people of Isaiah, we are unfaithful in our relationship with God. And like the nation of Israel during the time of Jeremiah, our nation has sought security in the horses and chariots of Egypt, instead of seeking security in the salvation of the Lord.

Today, we as a people are challenged to read the books of Amos, Hosea, Isaiah, and Jeremiah, and to discover how the Lord provides solutions to these problems through the messages of these prophets. And we as ministers to the people are challenged to provide messages that will both address the problems inherent in our society, and provide directions for resolving problems. It is my hope that the readers of this book will be inspired with new insights into the messages of Amos, Hosea, Isaiah, and Jeremiah, and that these insights will be reflected into new attitudes and behaviors in Christian living and meaningful approaches to new ministries in our society.

A Hunger That
Cannot Be Satisfied

Proper 11   *Amos 8:1-12*
Pentecost 9
Ordinary Time 16

What kind of hunger is so powerful, so insatiable that it cannot be satisfied? How does one describe such a hunger? How does one respond to it? The living examples of this type of hunger are all around us.

A young boy is lying on a cot in a dark room. He tosses and turns, fretting and frantic in a sleepless night. The room is warm, his stomach is full, but he is so hungry. He is sleeping on a bed, but it is not his bed. He is living with a family, but it is not his family.

His mother was killed in a domestic argument, and his father is in prison. He lives in his mother's sister's house, with his mother's sister's children. His eyes replay the scene of his mother's death over and over again. He was too young to stop his father from killing his mother, and he is too old to ever forget. And so he lives through sleepless nights and restless days. His stomach is full; his heart is hurting, from this hunger, this never ending hunger. It is *a hunger that cannot be satisfied.*

Let me give you another true life illustration. An old man rocks in his rocking chair in a quiet room. Familiar scenes of his family look back at him from the walls. But there are no voices, only pictures. He is safe and secure in this home, and he feels comfortable, but he does not feel at home. He is taken care of and well-fed. The nurse glances in every night to make sure that everything is all right. He wants to tell her that his body is all right in this nursing home, but his soul is in despair. This house just does not feel like his house, and these people do not feel like his family. There is comfort in his bones, but a hunger in his heart. It is *a hunger that cannot be satisfied.*

God dramatized this type of hunger to Amos in this Scripture. God showed Amos a basket of fruit. In Israel fruit was symbolic of a good harvest. Fruit represented plenty: plenty of corn, plenty of grain, plenty of fruit. But in the midst of this fruitfulness was a famine. He showed Amos that Israel was a dichotomy of fruit and famine, luxury and poverty, health and sickness. They had food, plenty of food, fruit from the trees and grapes from the vine, but the fruit was not good enough.

Surrounded by all of this fruitfulness there was still this hunger ... the people of Israel were starving to death. The rich were prosperous and the poor were starving to death. The powerful were taking advantage of the powerless, by forcing them to work as indentured servants to pay off their debts. Religion was prominent, but it had no moral content. Father and son were engaging in religious prostitution, and both were sleeping with the same woman.

God had given them everything that they needed. Amos reminds them of how the Lord brought them out of Egypt, how God brought them safely through the wilderness. God gave them this land flowing with milk and honey. Regardless of how well the Lord treated Israel, they always wanted more. Regardless of how much God blessed them, they were never satisfied. They had a hunger that could not be satisfied.

This unsatisfied hunger began to change Israel. It changed their relationship with God. They began to develop a negative attitude toward God. Where once they were a people who honored the Sabbath day, they became a people who could not wait for the Sabbath day to be over. They began to ask, "When will the service be over so that we can sell our crop and make our money?" They were a people who used holy days to give God thanks. They changed these holy days to holidays when they could give themselves entertainment and enjoyment.

It changed their relationship with each other. They went from being a caring people to a cutthroat people. They skimped the measure and boosted the price. They became a people that Amos described as "buying the poor with silver, and the needy for a pair of shoes."

An unsatisfied hunger will make people do strange things. It will make folks try to find love in the unloving. It will make folks try to make a home out of a hopeless situation. Abandoned babies will try to make a misfit into a mother, abandoned wives will try to make a heel into a husband. All because they have this *hunger that will not be satisfied.*

There is only one way our hunger can be satisfied. Amos identifies it when he says this is not a famine of food or of water, but a famine of hearing the word of God. How do you resolve a famine of hearing the word of God? First, you must realize that the reason that food cannot satisfy this hunger that is within you, that water cannot quench this thirst that is within you, that money cannot satisfy this hunger within you, is that *"Man does not live by bread alone, but by every word that proceeds out of the mouth of the creator"* (Matthew 4:4). If you are hungry, food won't fill you up, but God's word will. If you are lonely, people won't help you up, but God's word will. It took God's word to make you, and it takes God's word to keep you, and without God's word you will have this hunger in your life that *cannot be satisfied.*

Second, you must recognize that the famine is not on God's part. It is on our part. It is not a famine of receiving the word of God, but a famine of hearing the word of God. God is speaking to you. You have to decide if you want to *listen.*

Finally, you must turn this famine into a feast. The law of God has been given to us, but we have to read it. The word of God has been given to us, but we have to believe it. And the Son of God, who is the word made flesh, has died for us. All that we have to do is receive him. Then we don't have to worry about this hunger that is going on in our lives; we don't have to wonder about this hunger going on in our hearts. We can remember that Jesus said, "Blessed are those who hunger and thirst after righteousness, for they shall be *satisfied.*"

God Needs To
Save This Family

Proper 12   *Hosea 1:2-10*
Pentecost 10
Ordinary Time 17

There are many reasons why God needs to save the families described in this message. There are countless reasons why God needs to save any family. The primary reason is that we are unable to save our families ourselves. Let me illustrate a few scenes from modern American family life.

In the first scene, we see a white house on a corner with a picket fence all around it. A typical family event is occurring. The father slams the front door as he storms out of the house. The mother slams the bedroom door and falls across her bed crying. Her teenage daughter is lying across the couch, where she has fallen after her father knocked her down. The teenager came home from a party, just as her father came home from work. It was late, too late to be coming home, too late for excuses, almost too late for this family. In his anger the father hits his daughter, hard, too hard. There is some blood on his hands, and blood on her face, and some blood on the couch. And there are some tears, so many tears, and *so much anger.* Her little brother slips quietly to his room, falls on his knees, and whispers this little prayer: *"God needs to save this family."*

13

In the second scene, a choir is singing, in a little red brick A.M.E. church, and another family is coming together for worship. All of the family is together except the grandmother. The grandmother is with the family, but she is laying in a casket. His grandma is the only mother that the young boy facing the casket has ever known. His real mother is staring into the casket with a glazed look on her face. Her grief is lost somewhere between drinks, drugs, and depression. The boy isn't even sure that his mother knows where she is. He has never known where his father is, and the only other family that he has is his little sister, who is clinging to his arms. As the lid of the casket closes, a thought comes to his mind. "It was hard when grandma was alive; it will be impossible now that she's gone." This thought is followed by another thought, almost a prayer: "*God needs to save this family!*"

These illustrations are everyday situations in American life. They can be seen in any home. They can be heard on any street. They are a constant reminder to us that we are failing, failing in life, failing at the one thing that makes life most meaningful. We are failing to save our families. There can be no question that we need help, and that we are unable to help ourselves. We need God to help us save our families.

In this incident described by Hosea, we observe an example of God's direct involvement in the life of the family. God helps Hosea in the selection of a wife, and even helps Hosea in the naming of his children. In a word, the divine intervention that we seek in the life of our family is evident in the life of the family of Hosea.

But the result of God's intervention is not what we would have expected. This home of Hosea's is not a happy home. The wife of Hosea's is not a loving wife. And these children that Hosea is raising are not model children.

God tells Hosea to choose a woman of questionable lifestyle and corrupt morals. God tells Hosea to find a woman who sleeps around with other men and prostitutes her body. God tells Hosea to let this woman become his wife, and let this woman bear his children. When the children from this woman are born, they will be strange children. In fact, God tells Hosea, "You won't know who they are, and you won't be sure where they are coming from.

"You will have a son, and you will call him Jezreel, which means 'much seed has been planted.' But you won't be sure that this is your seed. You will have a daughter, and you will call her Lo-ruhamah, which means 'no mercy.' And from the day that this girl is born, she will have no mercy upon you. You will have a baby boy, and you will name him Lo-ammi, which means 'not my people.' He will not act like your people. He will not look like your people. You will not even be sure that he is your people."

And Hosea must have asked God, "Why are you doing this to me? I am a good man. I try to be a godly man. All I want to do is have a family and raise children. Why should I be married to the wrong woman? Why should I be forced to raise strange children?" He must have told God, "I am your prophet. Why do I have to suffer this way?" And God most certainly answered, "It is exactly because you are my prophet that you are living through this situation. Who else but my prophet could suffer like I suffer, and grieve like I grieve, and therefore understand what I understand? Hosea, because you agreed to be my prophet, I decided to let you understand how I feel about my people Israel. They abandoned me, the same way your wife abandoned you. Just as you can feel your grief, feel mine.

"You said that you wanted to know what God knows, and you wanted to feel what God feels. Well, Hosea, you are going to know exactly what I know, because you are going to live through what I live through. My people, Israel, have played the harlot on me, and given me strange children. And I want you, Hosea, to tell them how I feel. And you cannot tell them how I feel unless you have felt the same way. Hosea, I am giving you this experience so that you can feel my grief, and experience my pain, and know my hurt. Now you can tell my people how the Lord God feels when they grieve me and leave me to chase after other gods, and play the harlot with other nations."

In our neighborhoods, in our cities, and in our homes, like Hosea, we are producing strange families. We are choosing husbands and wives like Hosea did: wives who do not remain faithful to their husbands, and husbands who are running around on their wives.

As a result of our strange unions, our unfaithful marriages, we are producing strange children. We are raising sons like Jezreel, who think that it makes them a man to have a lot of children from a lot of different women. Having a child may make you a daddy, but it takes a lot more to become a FATHER.

We are raising daughters like Lo-ruhamah. Children who have no mercy. And because they have no mercy, they will steal from their fathers, fight their mothers, and kill their own brothers and sisters.

We are raising sons and daughters who must be named Lo-ammi, because they do not act like anybody in our family. They don't seem to love anybody in our family. We cannot even be sure that they are our family.

Like Hosea, we need to be asking, "Lord, what are you doing with our families?" And like the illustration of the little boy praying, we need to say a prayer, *"God needs to save our family!"*

If we look around us, don't we need to be saying, "God needs to save our family"? If we look at the condition of our society, we need to be praying, "God needs to save our family." And if we look at our own household, we need to be praying, *"God, you need to save our family!"*

Thank God that God does not allow us to get into anything that God cannot take us out of, especially when we belong to God. God's people may suffer through hardship, but God will take them through the hardship. God's people may fall upon hard times, but God will deliver them from the hard times. God's people have to climb up the rough side of the mountain, but my God will give them the strength to climb. Hosea suffered through his family situation, but God was with Hosea in the suffering.

God told Hosea, "The same way that I allowed your family to break down is the same way that I am going to build your family back up. Jezreel, the seed sower, will become Israel, the nation grower, for I will make him into a nation under God. Lo-ruhamah, the unmerciful, will become Ruhamah, full of mercy and grace. And I will make sisters love their brothers, and I will make brothers love their sisters. And Lo-ammi, who was named 'not my people,' will receive a new name. He will be called 'the children of the Living God.' And folks will say about your family, 'This is God's family,' and they will say about your children, 'These are God's children.' "

We need to thank God that he has the same message for us that he had for Hosea. God has given us a ministry to the family. It is a ministry of reconciliation and intercession. God has given us a ministry for the family. It is a ministry of repentance and forgiveness.

It is a ministry that tells husbands to hold on to their wives. If God brought you together, the same God will keep you together. It is a ministry that tells wives to forgive their husbands. I know your husband has not done everything right, but God knows that he didn't do everything wrong.

It is a ministry that tells parents to be reconciled with their children. Everything that you have tried to do for them may not have worked, but, believe me, you can work it out. The same God that gave them to you will help you raise them, if you ask him. God didn't give you perfect children, because he knew you were not a perfect parent. Yet God loved you, and as Romans 5:8 says, "While we were still sinners, Christ died for us." So, likewise, while our children are yet foolish, yet disobedient, let us pray for them, that God will do for them what God did for Hosea's children. God will take the bad seed Jezreel, and make him good seed Israel, and call him a child of God. God will take the hard, heartless, unmerciful child, and change him or her into a child of grace and mercy. God will take the one who does not act like us, who does not talk like us, and does not look like us, and God will change his ways, change his lifestyle, and change his demeanor. And people will look at our children and say that child acts just like his momma and daddy. He or she is a child of God.

We can't help ourselves. God needs to help us. We can't save this family. *God needs to save this family.*

God's Going To
Bring His Children Home

Proper 13   *Hosea 11:1-11*
Pentecost 11
Ordinary Time 18

In this family, there are four children, two boys and two girls. The oldest girl taught school, volunteered at the women's mission, and went to church every Sunday. The youngest girl kept a good house, raised five good children, never met a person she didn't like, and never met a person who didn't like her. The oldest boy followed his dad into missionary work, spent his youth in India feeding the hungry, and spent his manhood in South America building homes for the homeless. But the youngest son didn't like the teachings of his father and mother. He decided to get his teachings in the street, and find his spirits in a bottle.

For years the youngest son spent his nights in the streets, and his days in a drunken stupor. There was no place to go, nothing to do, nothing to live for. He moved from one lonely town to another lonely town in a lonely life. He looked down the dusty streets and watched the emptiness of people passing each other, and he felt like a stranger in a strange land.

One night he found himself in a strangely familiar town. He could see the outline of a distant steeple in the moonlight, and the voices of old memories spoke to him from the streets. In the distance he could hear the sound of a bell ringing in the city. Three

19

times the bell rang out its familiar song, six times it rang, twelve times, and then he remembered the name of the melody. He made his way around the corner to the building where the ringing was coming from, and made his way to the door. And when he looked up, he saw the choir singing the words to the song, "Amazing Grace, How Sweet The Sound." He made his way to the altar, and he recognized that he was in the same church, in the same town where his father and his mother raised him. It was New Year's Eve watch night service, and there was a sign above the altar: "God's Going To Bring His Children Home."

In this scripture, God is calling his children home, and God uses Hosea to call them home. Hosea understood what it meant for the family to be separated; he understood how it felt for husband to be separated from wife, parents to be separated from children. He had lived through this anguish with his own wife and suffered this separation from his own children, and he understood the anguish that God felt when God's people turned their backs on him.

That is why Hosea was given these words to describe the relationship between God and Israel: "When Israel was a child, then I loved him, and I called my son, out of Egypt." Hosea was speaking to kings, to governors, to priests, to soldiers, to the military academy of Israel, to the board of Israeli education, to organizations, and to institutions. And his words didn't make much sense, "When Israel was a child." How can a nation be a child?

With all of its land and institutions, how can a nation be a child? With the vast multitude of its people, how can a nation be a child? With its government, its political institutions, its vast array of organizations, how can a nation be a child? With hundreds of years of history behind it, how can a nation be a child?

God remembered this nation of Israel from its inception. God remembered when he conceived it through Abraham in Ur of the Chaldees. God remembered when he brought it forth like a newborn babe, in Goshen, when Moses took Israel out of Egypt. God nourished Israel at the Red Sea, and cared for it at the river of Jordan. God taught this nation to walk under Moses, and taught it to run and leap for joy under David.

And now this people, this nation that God had conceived and brought forth was acting childishly, and turning its back on God. So God had to find somebody who could understand what God felt and could describe, in a manner that these kings and priests, judges and farmers could understand, that God feels hurt and pain, just like a man feels hurt and pain. And so God gave these words to Hosea: "When Israel was a child, then I loved him, and I called my Son out of Egypt, but the more I called the more he ran from me."

This nation, this America, is just like a child to God. I know that we are a nation, with laws and governments and institutions, but to God we are just children. Barely 200 years old as a nation, we have not lived long enough to see everything and we have not been around long enough to understand everything. If we look at our 200 years of America in God's eyesight, aren't we just like children? We have a boys' clubhouse, where the girls are not allowed to come and play, and the results are female workers making less than male workers. Aren't we just like children? We have a team, where the fellows from one side of the street refuse to play with the fellows from another side of the street, because their hair is curly or their skin is dark. As a result, America has few Black-owned companies, and few Blacks in management. Aren't we just like children?

We as a people, African-American people, are acting just like children to God. I know that we are an ancient people, rooted in Africa, written about in the Bible, but when it comes to how we deal with each other and how we look to the world, we act just like children. We have thirteen-year-olds and fourteen-year-olds out in the street playing cops and robbers, but they are using real guns, and somebody is dying. Aren't we just like children? We have thirty-year-old women still dating like teenagers, and forty-year-old men still chasing skirts like young boys. Aren't we just like children? We don't create our own jobs; we don't develop our own goods; we don't provide for our own families; we don't even hire our own children. And since we don't provide for ourselves, we don't support ourselves, we don't develop ourselves, then we must

21

still be just like children. We have a nation full of adults who are still acting like children, *and it's time for us to grow up.*

Paul said, "When I was a child I spoke as a child, I acted as a child, but when I became a man, I put away childish things." America, it's time to put away childish things. African-Americans, it's time to put away childish things. Families, it's time to put away childish things. We need some wake-up calls. Martin Luther King was a wake-up call, and the million man march was a wake-up call. This word that God gave Hosea was a wake-up call. It was a wake-up call to a nation; it was a wake-up call to a people; it was a wake-up call to the family of Israel.

Sometimes a nation needs a wake-up call. God has been calling this nation for a long time. We have been running after money. We have been running after clothes. We have been running after a good time. And we have been running away from God. America, America, *God is going to bring his children home.*

Sometimes a people need a wake-up call. I know that we have excuses for the way that we act. We can blame the government; we can blame society. But the real reason for our condition is that as a people we have been running away from God. *God is going to bring his children home.*

Sometimes our families need a wake-up call. I know that there have been Jones and Smiths and Robinsons around for a long time, but no matter how long you have been here, to God your family is just a child. And God has been calling your family, telling them to come on back home. But, just like in Hosea, the more God called, the more your family has been running away from home. *Don't you know, God is going to bring your family home?*

There is a difference between calling somebody home and bringing them home. My parents used to call me home, first. Sometimes I ignored the call. Sometimes I resisted the call. Sometimes I delayed my response to the call. If the call didn't work, my parents found another way to bring me home. First, my parents would send someone out to find me. Finally, they would come to bring me home themselves.

God has sent out the call; now God is coming out to bring us home. It is different when God brings us home, because God is not man. There is atonement when God brings his children home. There is forgiveness when God brings his children home. There is reconciliation when God brings his children home. *God is going to bring his children home.*

Your Reflection
In God's Mirror

Proper 14   *Isaiah 1:1, 10-20*
Pentecost 12
Ordinary Time 19

In this first chapter of the book, Isaiah examines the nation of Judah as it looked during the reign of four kings: Uzziah, Jotham, Ahaz, and Hezekiah. As he examines them, he reflects on what Judah looks like when God looks at the nation. He tells Judah that when God looks at you, you don't look like yourself.

Your name is Judah, and you are the people of Jerusalem. Judah means the "praise of God," and you are the nation that was born in the praise of God. You are the people of Jerusalem, and Jerusalem is the holy city, but you don't look like a holy city.

Your relationship with God extends back to Abraham. Abraham left his mother's home, and his father's house, to follow God to an unknown land. Abraham was obedient to God. But when God looks at your reflection in his mirror, you don't look like an obedient people.

Your relationship with God extends back to Moses. Moses was raised in Egypt, in the "Big House," with Pharaoh's children. But when God asked Moses to give up the "Big House" and to lead his people out of Egypt, then Moses went to Pharaoh and told him, "God said, 'Let my people go.' " Moses had faith in God. But when God looks at your reflection in his mirror, you don't look like a faithful people.

Your relationship with God extends back to David. David was bold for the Lord. God took David from caring for sheep, and sent him to care for this people. And when the giant Goliath threatened God's people, David was so bold that he killed the giant with a slingshot in his hand. David was bold for the Lord, but when God looks at your reflection in his mirror, you don't look so bold.

When God makes a person God creates him or her in God's image, and after God's likeness. And when God creates a nation, God makes that nation to have some characteristics of their God. God is faithful and his nation should be faithful to God. God is righteous and there should be some righteousness in God's people. God is just, and his people should live by just laws in a just society. God is almighty, and his people should have some power.

But when God looked at Judah, God saw an unfaithful people. When God looked at Judah, God saw a people who did not live righteous lives. When God looked at Judah, God saw a people who were unfair and unjust. They had power because God gave them power, but they used their power to abuse and misuse each other.

So God sent Isaiah with this message to his people. He said, "This people doesn't look like Judah. They look like Sodom and they act like Gomorrah."

You remember Sodom. That is the place where people got captivated with sex. They became sexually permissive and sexually abusive. They began to sleep around with each other's wives, and soon they were abusing each other's children. They thought that they were sexually liberated, and became sexually perverse. Men began to lay with men, and women began to lay with women. After a while they did not know who they were or what they were.

You remember Gomorrah. That's where people got fascinated with violence. Men became abusive with their wives, and wives became disrespectful of their husbands. Parents abused their children and children disrespected their parents. And after a while they became so violent toward each other that they threatened to destroy each other.

You remember, God told Isaiah, "Because of their perversion and because of their violence I destroyed those cities. I wiped the memory of them from the face of the earth. I sent three angels to destroy those cities with their perversions and their abuses."

You remember, God told Isaiah, "I destroyed Sodom and Gomorrah, I made this nation called Judah after my image. I told them to live righteous lives and to perform just acts. But every time I look down at Judah, and every time I look at Jerusalem, they look just like Sodom and Gomorrah. And if they continue to look like Sodom, and to act like Gomorrah, I will do to them what I did to Sodom and Gomorrah. I will wipe them off the face of the earth."

America, oh America. You are beginning to look like Sodom, and you are beginning to act like Gomorrah. I know this is the land of the brave and the home of the free. I know that they sing of you, "My country 'tis of thee, sweet land of Liberty, of thee I sing." I know that this country was founded on the principle, "In God We Trust." But every time God looks down on America, God sees a nation captivated by sex and fascinated with violence. Every time God looks at America, God sees the violence of racism and the vice of sexism. Too many movies with violent content. Too many talk shows with perverse conversations and abusive language. And when God looks down at America, we don't look like America anymore, and we don't act like America anymore. We are beginning to look like Sodom and Gomorrah.

African-Americans, you used to hold a standard for strong families and strict morals. You had strong family ties and extended family principles that caused you to treat each other like brothers. You seem to have forgotten your morals and deserted your religion. You have abandoned your children and deserted your families. And now when God looks at Black America, you look like Sodom and you act like Gomorrah.

God has an image that God expects us to reflect. God has a standard that God expects us to uphold. God has a mirror, and God expects us to become a mirror image of God's love and a mirror image of God's morality. God has placed his image in us, and God expects us to reflect his image. God has placed his words in us and

27

God expects us to live according to his words. God's words are in God's book; God's book is our Bible. And if we don't live according to God's word, if we don't live according to the Bible, then we can't reflect God's image.

Isaiah had some bad news, but he also had some good news. There was a way for Judah to become whole again. He told them, "Wash yourselves; make yourselves clean. Be clean on the inside and be clean on the outside." He tells us today, "Wash yourself; make yourself clean." We need to be clean on the outside, baptized with the water of baptism. We need to be clean on the inside, baptized with the Holy Ghost.

Isaiah has some good news for us. "Cease to do evil; learn to do good. Seek justice, correct oppression; defend the fatherless ... plead for the widow." After we have made ourselves clean, then God himself will clean us up. "Come, let us reason together," says the Lord. "Though your sins are as scarlet, I will make them as white as snow."

You need to look at yourself in God's mirror. I know that you have your own opinion of yourself, but you need to look at yourself in God's mirror. We need to look at ourselves as a nation. We need to look at ourselves as a people. We need to look at ourselves as the people of God. We need to see ourselves as God sees us. There are some Judah folk that look like Sodom. There are some Jerusalem folk that are acting like Gomorrah. But God has an answer for us. God says, "Come, let us reason together, though your sins are like scarlet, they shall be as white as snow."

A Christian With
A Conflict Of Interest

Proper 15   **Isaiah 5:1-7**
Pentecost 13
Ordinary Time 20

This was a Christian family. The husband was a Christian, at least that is what he put on his job application when it asked for religious affiliation.

Sex: male   Race: African-American
Nationality: U.S. Citizen   Religion: Christian

His mother has been a good churchwoman. He used to attend Sunday school as a little boy, but that was thirty years ago. He had a religious heritage and, after all, that made him Christian by parental relationships. Or did it?

He wanted to think of himself as a Christian every day, except Thursday. Thursday was happy days at happy hour. And maybe Friday, because payday was Friday, and everybody knows, "Friday the eagle flies, and Saturday I go out to play." Sunday was a good day, but it wasn't a church day. He had to rest Sunday from Thursday, Friday, and Saturday. He thought about church, but as he looked at himself he was a good man. He didn't understand that his good just wasn't good enough. He was a Christian, but he had this conflict of interest.

His wife was a Christian woman. At least she did Christian things. She went to church on Sunday, clapped her hands on Sunday.

29

But she talked about people all day Monday. She said it was because she was always home, always alone. She complained about her job, she complained about her husband, sometimes she even complained about the Lord. She said she was just trying to get the Lord's attention, but Saturday she was trying to get the attention of available men. She claimed that she wasn't the best person, but she wasn't the worst person. She was a Christian, but she had this conflict of interest.

The child of this dynamic duo was a desperate child. He was in-between, in-between childhood and adulthood, in-between believing his parents and following his friends, in-between faith in the church and fun in the streets. He was questioning who this God was, but he didn't want to question too loud. He didn't want his friends to think that he was too strange, or too religious, or too square, or too different. He told himself that what he was doing wasn't too bad, after all everyone else was doing it. He was still a Christian, he just had this conflict of interest.

Isaiah was describing this conflict through the analogy of a grapevine. The vinekeeper cleared the land, and he removed all the stone. He planted the vine in the middle of a fruitful hill. He placed a watchtower near the vine so that he could watch over it. He put a wine vat nearby so that he could harvest its fruit. When it came time for the vine to produce grapes, it produced wild grapes. The fruit from the vine looked like grapes. When you tasted the fruit to enjoy its sweetness, however, it was not sweet like a grape. It tasted like wild grapes that grow in the wilderness.

The Lord was telling Jerusalem, and the men of Judah, "I placed you in the middle of a fruitful hill. And I placed my word in a watchtower so that it could watch over you. I placed my temple nearby so that I could receive the fruit of my labor when you served me in my temple. But when it came time to taste the sweetness of your attitude, the kindness of your words, the joy of your spirit, it turned out that you were not very sweet after all. Your attitude was bitter, not sweet, and your words were harsh and not kind. Your spirit was mean and not joyful. You looked like God's people, you even said the words that God's people should say, you sounded like God's people. But when it came time for godly acts, you acted

30

ungodly. Maybe you are my people, but you have this conflict of interest."

The apostle Paul identifies this characteristic in Romans 7:18-19: "I know that nothing good lives in me, that is, in my sinful nature. For I have the desire to do what is good, but I cannot carry it out. For what I do is not the good that I want to do; no, the evil I do not want to do — this I keep on doing."

Paul was saying, "I want to do right, but I keep on doing wrong. I keep running into this conflict. Conflict all around me, conflict inside me. I am trying to be a Christian, but I have a conflict of interest."

There are things that I should do. I should go to church on Sunday, but Sunday conflicts with my rest time, and my play time, and my personal time. I should read my Bible more often, but Bible study conflicts with my rest time. I should go to Sunday school, but that would conflict with my rest time. Sunday is the only morning that I have to rest. But if you can get up to go to your job during the week, then you can get up to serve your God Sunday. I would go to prayer meeting, but those people get too holy. Don't you know that if you don't want to talk to God on your time, God may not want to talk to you on his time? I know that I should give my tithes to the church, but the church is always asking for money. If the doctor asks for money, that's all right. If the bill collector asks for money, you say, "I've got to pay my bills." If you shop at the mall, and the stores raise their prices, you say, "It's my money; I spend it the way I like." But when God asks for money, you say, "How dare God ask for the little bit of money that I have left!" Don't you know that all the money that you have comes from God? And sometimes God gives it to you to test you, to see if you are willing to give ten percent back to him.

Then, there are things that you said you would not do, but you still do. You said that cigarettes were ruining your health, and you were going to give them up. You said that you were drinking too much. You were getting up in the morning with a drink, and going to bed at night with a drink, and you were still trying to say that you are just a social drinker. The problem is that now you don't know how to be sociable without a drink, and you don't act too sociable with a drink. You said that you would stop fussing with the wife, and stop yelling at the kids. You said that you could not build your home, if you kept running the streets. But every time you try to stop doing wrong, you find yourself in conflict, and every time you try to do right, you find yourself in conflict. And you are trying to be a Christian, but you have this conflict of interest.

Well, Christians, there are three things that you must do to overcome your conflict. You must confront the conflict, then you must correct the conflict, and finally you must crucify the conflict. First, you must confront the conflict. You cannot remove something if you deny that it is there. If you deny that you have bad habits, bad attitudes, or bad behavior, then you will just deceive yourself. But you won't deceive anyone else. You must admit that you can't control your emotions. You have to acknowledge that there is a conflict between how you act and how you want to act. Then you must face this conflict, confront it with yourself.

Second, you must take the steps to correct the conflict. You must realize that you must change and be willing to start to change. If every time someone disagrees with you, you blow up with an explosive temper, then you must calm yourself, correct yourself, and stop the explosion. If every time something happens that you don't understand you become suspicious and jump to conclusions, then you must slow yourself down, sit yourself down, and think about what you have seen and heard, before you jump to conclusions.

I realize that many of you have tried to confront your conflict. You have recognized that you have a problem, and taken the steps to confront your problem. Some of you have even taken steps to correct your problem. You have tried to stop doing what you were doing, tried to stop saying what you were saying. You have taken therapy and counseling, tried behavior modification and self-help courses. And despite what you have tried, or how often you have tried, you find that you have failed. That is because you have taken two steps, but you haven't taken the final step. You must crucify the conflict on the cross. When I say crucify the conflict, that means you have to give it to Jesus. When you can't control your anger,

32

give it to Jesus. When you can't control that habit, give it to Jesus. When you can't control your life, give it to Jesus. Maybe you can't handle it, but God can. "If you have the faith, He's got the power." Listen to the words of Romans 6:6-7: "For we know that our old self was crucified with him so that the body of sin might be done away with, that we should no longer be slaves to sin — because anyone who has died has been freed from sin."

And when you crucify your conflict on the cross of Jesus, you become transformed. In the words of Romans 12:1-2: "Therefore, I urge you, brothers, in view of God's mercy, to offer your bodies as living sacrifices, holy and pleasing to God — this is your spiritual act of worship. Do not conform any longer to the pattern of this world, but be transformed by the renewing of your mind. Then you will be able to test and approve what God's will is — his good, pleasing, and perfect will."

Confront your conflict. Correct your ways. Crucify your desires on the cross. Your conflict will die, but your spirit will rise again. And then you will become a Christian, with no conflict of interest.

You Need A Point Of Contact
With The Lord

Proper 16   *Jeremiah 1:4-10*
Pentecost 14
Ordinary Time 21

Let me describe how important a point of contact is. An experiment was performed on some baby monkeys. The baby monkeys were placed in a wire cage with two surrogate mothers: a wire imitation mother with a milk bottle, and a cloth mother with no food. The experiment was trying to determine to which of these mothers the infant monkeys would go. The monkeys fooled the experimenters. They went to the wire mother with the milk when they were hungry, but they spent the rest of their time with the cloth mother. The experimenters concluded that although the baby monkeys needed the milk, they spent most of the time with the cloth mother, because they also needed a point of contact.

Every mother knows that when an infant cries in the night, and the diaper is not wet, and the baby has been fed, and the bed is cuddly, and the room is warm, the baby is not crying because he or she needs anything. The baby is crying because he or she needs a point of human contact. Ask young men or young women who have spent their first month away from home in the army, in a college, or in a marriage. Though they couldn't wait to be away from home on their own, they will call home every day, send letters,

35

and drive hundreds of miles on the weekends. The reason is that they miss that point of human contact.

It takes a point of contact between a husband and a wife to make a marriage work. You can have a nice home, two cars, and money in the bank, but if there is no time when husband and wife spend time together, if there is no place where husband and wife get together, in other words, if there is no point of contact, then there is no relationship, and you don't have a marriage, you have an arrangement.

It takes a point of contact between parents and their children to make a family. Fathers have to spend time with their sons, and mothers have to spend time with their daughters, and brothers have to spend time with sisters, and sisters have to spend time with brothers. If there is no point of contact, then there is no relationship, and you don't have a family. You just have a house that is not a home. And more importantly, in fact, most importantly, if you are going to live this life that God gave you in this world that God created, then you need a point of contact with the Lord.

In Jeremiah 1:4-10, Jeremiah discovered that he had been in contact with the Lord. The first thing he realized was that God had been in contact with him from the beginning. The Lord said to Jeremiah, "Before I formed you in the belly, I knew you, and before you came out of the womb, I consecrated you."

God was saying to him, "Before I formed you, I knew you." This Hebrew word for forming, *yetzar*, is the same word used in Genesis 2:7, when it says God formed man out of the dust of the ground. It means to shape out, to squeeze, to mold, to make. It means to take nothing, and make something out of it. God was telling Jeremiah that when you were nothing, I knew what you were, and I made something out of you.

God also told Jeremiah, "Before you came out of the womb, I consecrated you." The Hebrew word for consecrate is *qadosh*, to make clean, to purify, to make holy. He was telling Jeremiah, "After I formed you, I purified you, I made you clean, I made you whole." In other words, God was telling Jeremiah, "I was in contact with you at birth, I was in contact with you while you were in the womb, and I was still in contact with you when you came out of the womb. I have had a *point of contact with you from the very beginning.*"

Secondly, we must realize that this contact did not occur through Jeremiah's efforts. Jeremiah was not even aware of this contact. God had to reveal this contact to him. God was in contact with Jeremiah, but Jeremiah had no contact with God. Jeremiah did not know how he was formed. He did not remember his condition in his mother's womb. He didn't know that God had squeezed him out and cleaned him up.

So this contact was one-sided. God knew Jeremiah, but Jeremiah didn't know God. God had done everything for Jeremiah, but Jeremiah had not done anything for the Lord. Jeremiah's reaction to this one-sided relationship was, "I do not know how to speak, but I am a boy." I do not know what to do, Lord, because I am just my mother's child.

God responded to Jeremiah with these words: "Wherever I send you, you shall go, whatever I command you, you shall speak." That is, "I know that you are grown, and you are used to going your own way, Jeremiah, but if I send you East, and you try to go West, your head will point in one direction, and your feet will move in another. I know that you are an adult, and you have your own mind, and you can speak your own tongue, but after the Lord gets ahold of you, you will start out cursing, and you will end up saying, 'Praise the Lord.' "

Sometimes God has to reestablish contact with his people. This is what God did with Jeremiah in this text. God reached forth his hand and placed his hand on Jeremiah's mouth, and Jeremiah discovered that he was in contact with the Lord. God told Jeremiah, "You don't have to worry about what you are going to say; I have put my words in your mouth." God told Jeremiah, "You don't have to worry about where you are going to go; I have placed you over nations, and put you in charge of kingdoms." God told Jeremiah, "You don't even have to worry about what you are going to do when you get to the kingdoms of men. I'll tell you which ones to uproot, I'll tell you which ones to tear down, I'll show you what people to build up, and I'll show you which people to plant. And don't be afraid of them, don't be afraid of their faces, or of their ways, for 'I will be with you to deliver you,' " says the Lord.

Each one of us needs a point of contact with the Lord. God has been in contact with us; we need to get in contact with the Lord. When we get up in the morning, we need a point of contact with the Lord. When we get ready to go to school, we need a point of contact with the Lord. Before we go to work, we need to get in contact with the Lord.

Now there is a way to get in contact with the Lord. You can say: "Lord, touch my mouth. 'Let the words of my mouth, and the meditation of my heart be acceptable in thy sight.' " You can say, "Lord, touch my feet. 'Thy word is a light upon my way, and a lamp unto my feet.' " You can say, "Lord, touch my hands. 'Establish thou the works of my hands.' " Whatever you say, whatever you do, you need a point of contact with the Lord.

How To Find Water
When Your Well Runs Dry!

Proper 17   *Jeremiah 2:4-13*
Pentecost 15
Ordinary Time 22

First, we must establish and explain to you that most of the water you drink comes from a well. Your fathers and mothers and grandparents were well acquainted with this fact, because most of them were born on a farm.

On a farm, you had to find a source of water before you built a house, because land had no value if it did not have a well. Well water was always located below the surface. The farmer had to select a good site, dig a deep cistern (a man-made hole), and tap the well springs of underground water. The farmer enlarged the hole, built walls around it, and placed a bucket at the top, so that he could draw water from the bottom. He called this completed system a well.

Most of us no longer live on farms, but we still drink water from a well. We build bigger wells. We call them reservoirs, and we place them on the outskirts of the city. But instead of buckets, we take pipes and connect them on one end to our homes, and on the other end to the well of water in the reservoir.

In this well water system, there was always a problem if the well ran dry. If the well was not deep enough, then sometimes the well would run dry. If the walls of the well were not built firmly enough, then sometimes the walls of the well would collapse, and the well would run dry. If it did not rain hard enough, or long enough, or often enough, then the water in the ground would dry up, and the well would run dry.

America, oh America, we have some dry water systems in our society. We have let down our buckets into the mainstreams of our society, and when we lift them up, we find that there is no more water in the well. Our well has run dry.

Our people are not healthy. We have a nation with the most advanced scientific technology developing the greatest medical discoveries. But some of our elderly are paying fifty percent of their income for hospital bills and prescription medicine, and making decisions between buying food and buying medicine, staying healthy or staying alive. In the midst of this medical dilemma, politicians are planning major cuts in Medicare for the elderly. The system is in place, but every time we let down our buckets, the well is running dry.

Our children are not being educated. We have more public schools, more colleges and universities than any nation in the world. But we have one of the highest dropout rates of any country. Our illiteracy rate is above that of some third world countries. And our children who attend school are unable to pass the mathematics and English proficiency tests. In the midst of all this, our national government is proposing cuts in the school lunch program, our state government is cutting funds for higher education, and our local school systems are expelling and suspending more students from our schools. The system is in place, but every time we let down our buckets, the well is running dry.

We are losing our sources of employment, and our people are losing their jobs. Factory shutdowns have turned steel industries into rust belts. Factory relocations have split families, isolated friends, and turned large cities into small towns. American workers, once industrial workers with top pay and good benefits, are now service workers with longer hours, less pay, and no benefits. The system is in place, but when we let down our buckets, the well is running dry.

In the midst of this breakdown of systems, there is one system meant to remain. When all other systems run dry, the church has a deep well, a reservoir of living water, that all other systems can turn to. The church is a system that can never run dry. But when the sick come, and the poor come, and the uneducated come to the church, and put down their buckets into the wellsprings of the church, they are coming up with empty buckets.

The form is there, but often it is form without content. The building looks good. The people dress good. The service sounds good. But when you dig beneath the surface, and reach down into that well where good character should produce good works, there is no water in the well, and the well has run dry.

The fashion is there, but it's fashion without substance. The choir is singing, but they are not listening to the words of their song. The ushers are serving, but they are not feeling the sacredness of their service. The preacher is preaching to the people, but the people are not listening to his words. There is a well, but there is no water in the well. The well has run dry.

In this text, Jeremiah addresses the mistakes of a religious people, living in a religious society. He tells them they have deserted the God that they were devoted to, they have turned away the firstfruits of their offerings, and their well has run dry.

"Two sins my people have committed," says Jeremiah. "They have forsaken the spring of living water, and have dug their own cisterns (they have dug their own wells), broken cisterns that cannot hold water." We know about the broken cisterns; broken cisterns are wells that cannot hold water. We have created our own cisterns.

We believed that money was all we needed, but when the money ran out, we found out that was a broken cistern, which cannot hold water. We believed that the government would take care of us, but when government betrayed us, we found out that sometimes government is a broken cistern, which cannot hold water. We believed in friends, and friends betrayed us; we believed in family, and family deserted us; we believed in ourselves, but we could not deliver ourselves. And we discovered that we have these broken cisterns, and they cannot hold water. And while we believed these things,

41

we had turned our backs on the spring of living water. You may ask: What is the spring of living water?

There was a spring of living water in Exodus 17:1. Moses was in the wilderness and there was no water for the people to drink. And God told Moses to strike the rock, and water came out of the rock. There was a spring of living water in Psalm 1:3. David described the righteous man. He said, "And he shall be like a tree, planted by the rivers of water."

In John 4:13-14, Jesus was at a well and he gave an answer about the water to the woman of Samaria. Jesus said, "Everyone who drinks of this water will be thirsty again, but whoever drinks the water that I give him will never thirst. Indeed, the water that I give him will become in him a spring of water welling up to eternal life."

One day, on Calvary, when the well of the world was dry, Jesus made a new source of well water for the world. They pierced him in the side, and out of the wound came blood mixed with water. The songwriter had this to say about it: "There is a fountain filled with blood, drawn from Immanuel's vein, and sinners, plunged beneath the flood, lose all their guilty stain."

This is the water. This is the wellspring of eternal life. This is the water that supplies the life to our church, so that the church can provide the spirit of life to the community. But the question still remains: How do we find the water when the well runs dry? We know where the water is; how do we find it? We need three things: discipleship, stewardship, and fellowship of the Spirit.

First, we must develop discipleship. Jeremiah 2:1 talks about discipleship. In discipleship you must be devoted. You must read the word, do the work, and change the world. In discipleship you must love. It's easy enough to love everybody in the church. You have to learn to love everybody in the world. In discipleship you must follow the Lord. Don't just worship the Lord; follow the Lord. Don't just love the Lord; follow the Lord. That is what discipleship means, followers. And when you follow him, you can locate the water when the well runs dry.

Second, you must strive for stewardship. Jeremiah 2:3 talks about stewardship. In stewardship you must learn to give your firstfruits. You give to the church because you love the Lord. How can you love somebody that you don't support? Husbands, how can you love your wives and not support them? Parents, how can you love your children and not support their schools? Christians, how can you love the Lord, and not support the Church? And when you strive for stewardship, you can build the walls of the well, so the well won't run dry.

Third, you must have fellowship in the Holy Spirit. Jeremiah 2:1 and 2:4 says, "The word of the Lord came to me, and told me to proclaim to you." Finally, it says, "Hear the word of the Lord." Fellowship means God speaks to me, and I speak to you. Fellowship means I give you God's word, and you take God's word and give it to somebody else, who takes it and gives it to somebody else. Fellowship means you hear the word of God and you obey. And when you are in fellowship in the Holy Spirit, you have located the water, you have dug the well, and now it's time to dip the bucket down into the deep, deep down into the spirit, deep down below the surface. And when your bucket comes up, there will be water in the bucket; your well is not dry. And then you will know how to find water when your well runs dry.

Go Down To
The Potter's House

Proper 18   *Jeremiah 18:1-11*
Pentecost 16
Ordinary Time 23

What is meant when we say, "Go down to the potter's house"? Let me explain through these illustrations.

A young mechanic was doing his studies about engine repair. He was in the final stages and was discussing with his instructor what he felt was the most important thing he needed to learn to master the engine. He told his instructor that he had read all of the relevant material on the internal combustion engine, the rotary engine, and turbochargers. He stated that he knew that the engine has nine systems, just like the human body: the oil system, the cooling system, the fuel system, the exhaust system, the electrical system, the drive train system, the steering system, the suspension system, and the braking system. He told his instructor that, if needed, he could enumerate the laws of thermodynamics and thermal electric power. The instructor reached out his hand, and the young mechanic, thinking that he was about to be congratulated, quickly placed his hand in the instructor's hands. As the instructor grasped his hand, he felt the fingers to see if there were any calluses, and he felt the palms, and they were as soft as a baby's skin. The instructor grasped the young mechanic's hands, briskly pulled him close, and whispered in his ear. "If you really want to be a mechanic,

45

let me give you a piece of advice. Go down to the auto shop and wrap your hands around an engine, and stick your fingers in some grease, and then you will know what it means to become a master mechanic."

A young college student wanted to know everything she needed to be a master in addressing social problems. As she met with her advisor, she discussed her training in sociology and the grades she had obtained in human psychology. She told him that she understood Freud's theory of personality, and that she could identify and describe Erik Erikson's eight-stages of human growth and development: she knew about trust vs. mistrust, autonomy vs. shame and doubt, initiative vs. guilt, industry vs. inferiority, identity vs. role confusion, intimacy vs. isolation, generativity vs. stagnation, and integrity vs. despair. The advisor looked in the young woman's eyes and he saw the intensity of her dedication and the sincerity of her commitment. Then he took out his notepad and wrote down these words. "You have learned all the theory, and you have received all the training. The only thing that you need is to come in contact with human problems. Go down to the neighborhood center and touch the lives of boys and girls, men and women, and after you give them all that you have in you, then they will give you all that you need to address human problems."

In this text, God was preparing Jeremiah to receive his message, and the first thing God told him was you have to "go down...." There was not going to be any isolation in quiet rooms, no separation from people, no immersing oneself in meditation, no studious survey of books, to prepare this sermon. God told Jeremiah that in order to understand this message he would have to "go down ... go down from your high studies, go down from your proper priestly position, go down from your isolation, go down...."

Sometimes, Christians, we are seeking to understand the healing power of prayer. In order to understand it, we read the right prayer books, and we study the correct prayer meditations, and we learn the types of prayer, and we rehearse prayer techniques. All of this is good for a beginning, but it is only a beginning. In order to understand the healing power of prayer, we have to go down ... go down to a hospital, and pray for somebody who is sick. If we have come down enough from our pinnacle of piety, and we let God work, we will see the healing power of prayer at work, and we will understand that God is a healer. In fact, we will see that God is *the* healer. God will hear our prayer and heal somebody, if we only go down where people need us to pray.

Sometimes we Christians are seeking to understand the deliverance power of preaching. All we need to do is go down to the prisons, go down to the homeless, go down to the streets, and proclaim the word of God. Somebody will hear us and be delivered; someone will follow us, and be saved, if we will only go down....

Jeremiah was preparing God's message, and God told him that in order to prepare this sermon he must "go down to the potter's house...." In Jeremiah's day, you couldn't cook a meal unless you went down to the potter's house. You couldn't carry water from a well unless you went down to the potter's house. To beautify your house, to plant flowers in a vase, you had to go down to the potter's house. And God's message to Jeremiah was, "If you want to understand who I am, Jeremiah, you have to go down to the potter's house."

The potter's house was called the *Bayith Ytsar*, the house of molding or making, because the potter would take the clay and mold it and make it, and give form to that which had no form. When God made man, the description given in Genesis 2:7 is that the Lord God formed the man. This same word "form," in the Hebrew, *ytzar*, means that God took clay, like a potter, and molded the man into God's own image, just as the potter molds and makes the clay into pottery.

When Jeremiah reached the potter's house, he saw the potter working at the wheel, but the pot that he was working on was marred, and the potter took the clay and formed it into a new pot. God told Jeremiah, "My people are just like that clay. They have been marred and broken, and they refuse to be remade." But the potter can take old clay and make a new thing. All that we have to do is "go down to the potter's house."

I know that each one of you is already fixed in your ways and fixed in your habits. I know that you are used to doing things the way that you do them and saying things the way that you say them.

And I know that if you don't want to change, nobody is going to make you change. But I just want to tell you that I've got this message for you: "Go down to the potter's house ... There is somebody down at the potter's house sitting at a wheel, who can change you and rearrange you...."

It's a new year, but if we do the same things this year that we did last year, then we are going to get the same results. I've got a new year's message for you: "Go down to the potter's house." There is somebody down at the potter's house that can take old clay and do a new thing.

Some of you have been broken by life, and marred by circumstances, and damaged by situations, until the vessel that contains your life cannot hold substance anymore. I've got a message of hope for you: "Go down to the potter's house." The Lord is down there, and he can take your brokenness and fix it; he can take your marred condition, and heal it. All you have to do is "go down to the potter's house."

Lord, Send
The Wind

Proper 19
Pentecost 17
Ordinary Time 24

Jeremiah 4:11-12, 22-28

What does it mean to ask the Lord to send the Wind? Let me give you some examples.

Together four eyes peered into the vacant alley of an overcrowded apartment complex. They wiped sweat from their faces as they watched the red sun of a hot day dip below the horizon, only to reveal the white moon of a hotter night. Next door through the paper-thin walls, they could hear a man and a woman arguing about the night before and the night before that. Upstairs, through the hollow ceiling they could hear the cries of abandoned children left to swelter alone in the hot night. There was no relief from the heat, and there was no relief from the angry emotions. The brothers' eyes looked on each other, and their hands locked together, as both mouthed the words of a silent prayer, *"Lord, send the Wind."*

Husband and wife sat in a small kitchen of a smaller apartment. No water, no electricity, no heat; the room was lit by candlelight. Envelopes filled with bills were piled on the table and on the floor. Husband and wife sat in the same room, but they were not together. Neither one wanted to leave; neither one wanted to stay. Money problems, family problems, and employment problems had heated up an already hot relationship. The man looked up from the

Holy Bible open on the table before him and reached his hand across the table to grab her hand. With a tear in his eye, he said a quiet prayer: *"Lord, send the Wind."*

The ancient Hebrews had a strong belief about the wind. It was the wind that provided relief from the hot desert sun. It was the wind that supplied the power for movement from one environment to another environment, from stagnant conditions to better possibilities. It was the wind that not only came from God, but also was the Spirit of God. The word for spirit, *ruach*, was the same word for wind. And in the beginning, according to Genesis 1:2, when the spirit of God hovered over the face of the waters, and God created the heaven and earth in seven days, he accomplished this by his wind, his breath, the Holy Spirit.

In this scripture text, when Jeremiah looked at the situation of the people of Judah, he saw that God was preparing once again to send the wind upon his people. But this wind was not a cool breeze to drive away the heat; it was a hot blast of God's anger.

This wind would not be followed by the rain to wash away the filth and the grime. This would be a dry wind of judgment. This wind was not the Spirit of Creation in Genesis 1:2, but the Spirit of Destruction of Jeremiah 4:22. When Jeremiah looked at the results of this wind, he said, "I looked at the earth and it was formless and empty. I looked at the mountains and they were quaking. I looked and there were no people. I looked and the fruitful land was a desert."

Judah and Jerusalem that Jeremiah loved would never be the same again, after the coming of the Lord's Wind. But God has a reason for sending the Wind. Even when the Wind seems to bring destruction, if the Lord sends the Wind, it's the preparation for another creation.

After God sent the Wind, the land changed. The people of Judah lost their land and were sent into captivity in Babylon. The city of Jerusalem was destroyed, but God reached down into Babylon and brought his people back home to the Promised Land. And where there used to be an old Jerusalem, he built a new Jerusalem. After God sent the Wind, the leadership changed. Israel never had another prophet like Moses or another king like David. But God sent another kind of leadership. Down in a small town of this small nation, God sent a little baby, and they called his name Jesus, because he would save his people from their sins.

Sometimes, in order to move people past their old bad habits, and past their old repetitive sins, and past their old wicked ways, God has to shake up some mountains. God has to empty some places that used to be full. God has to take away some blessings and leave a barren land. Sometimes God has to send the Wind.

Our society, like Jeremiah's society, seems to be locked into old habits. The rich get richer, and the poor keep getting poorer. Immorality is rampant. Lust, sex, and violence have become fixed in the core of our society and in the hearts of our people. Corruption is not decreasing; it is increasing. Our people, like Jeremiah's people, seem to be fixed in their ways. Everybody wants things to change; nobody is willing to be changed. And the church, the house of God, has become so apathetic, so complacent. We seem to have adopted an attitude of business as usual. But the situation that this society is locked into is not a usual situation, and, thank God, our God is not a usual God.

We refuse to shake ourselves up, and we refuse to wake the world up, so God is going to have to break up this stagnant condition and "send the Wind." The Lord is going to send the Wind.

There is something peculiar about God's Wind; there is something moving about God's Wind. In the book of Acts 2:2, there was a dying world and a complacent people of God, and then God sent his Wind. The description says, "They were all gathered together in one place. Suddenly a sound like the blowing of a violent wind came from heaven and filled the whole house where they were sitting ... and all of them were filled with the Holy Spirit."

Today in God's church, and in God's world, again, God needs to "send the Wind."

Is This The Season
To Seek Salvation?

Proper 20   *Jeremiah 8:18—9:1*
Pentecost 18
Ordinary Time 25

The harvest is past, the summer is ended, and we are not saved
(Jeremiah 8:20).

Friends and Family, Family and Friends, the Lord sent me to
ask you this question: "Is this the season to seek salvation?"

A single mother had to ask this question concerning her teenage daughter. At age eleven, her daughter began to ask questions
about God. She told her mother she wanted to go to church. But
her mother wasn't religious and did not see any reason why her
teenage daughter should be so religious. So she kept her out of
church, but she couldn't keep her from the parties. Two years later
at age thirteen, her young daughter had a baby. As she looked at
her teenage daughter, the mother had to ask herself this question,
"Did I miss the season to seek salvation?"

A young man had to ask this question concerning his family.
The young man was 25, raising a good family. The woman was a
good wife for a good husband. He had no faults, except that he
worked all the time. He was trying to excel in his job so that he
could build up his home and take care of his family. He never had
time for church. He believed in God, but he also believed that he
would have time for God after a while — after he got his

53

promotions, after he built his new home, after his family was settled. But one day before he got his life together, time and circumstances tore his life apart. A driver missed a brake pedal, and his car went out of control. The car struck the young man, paralyzing his body from the waist down. As he was lying in the hospital bed, he had this thought: "Is this the season to seek salvation?"

Ecclesiastes 3:1 says, "To everything there is a season." In our marriages, we have seen a season of disruption and divorce, broken homes and broken hearts. Maybe we need a season of salvation. In our families, we have seen a season of division and despair, abandoned children and abandoned wives. Maybe we need a season of salvation. In our streets, we have seen a season of violence and death; the death that once was prevalent among the old is now prevalent among the young. Maybe we need a season of salvation. Even in our churches, we have seen a season of apathy and despair. We no longer are winning the battle against sin and the war against evil. We're not winning the battle, and we are losing the war. Maybe, just maybe, we need a season of salvation.

The book of Jeremiah tells a tale of the seasons of a man. The seasons of a man are childhood, youth, maturity, and old age. Sometime in childhood we are supposed to learn about the Lord, so that we can begin to understand that the same God who made this world made us and provided for us all that we have and all that we need. Sometime in youth we are supposed to learn to love the Lord, just as we learn to love our father and our mother, our sisters and our brothers. We learn to love the Lord who gave us our family and included us in his family through Jesus. And then sometime in our maturity we are supposed to learn how to serve the Lord. As we appreciate what God has done for us, we begin to do things for him. As God has given to us, we learn to give to him. Then in our old age we can have joy in the presence of the Lord. We can then stand firm in the faith that God is with us and that, as the songwriter wrote, "He is very present help in the time of trouble."

But in Jeremiah chapter 8, something has gone wrong with the seasons. In verse 13, God tells Jeremiah, "There will be no grapes on the vine, there will be no figs on the trees, and their leaves will wither."

In verse 20, we find out what is wrong: "The harvest is past, the summer has ended, and we are not saved." There is something very special about the harvest. The harvest is the culmination of all the seasons that precede it, and the preparation for all the seasons that follow it. The reason that there is the season of Spring is so that the seed that is planted in spring will become fruit for the harvest. The reason that there is the season of Summer is so that the fruit will become ripe, and the vegetables will reach maturity. The reason that there is the season of Fall is so that the fruit can be picked, and the vegetables can be gathered, and then there will be food in the storehouse for winter.

But if there is no harvest, then all the work of spring was done in vain. If there is no harvest, then all the crops of summer have not grown ripe. If there is no harvest, then the winter will be long and cold and hungry.

Jeremiah was trying to teach the people of God about a spiritual harvest. God had given them a spiritual Spring, and God had planted his word in their hearts. God had given them a Summer, and the word of God had become the works of God. Now it was time to reap the harvest, but nobody was being saved. "The harvest was past, the summer was ended, and they were not saved."

We need to look at our day, like Jeremiah looked at his day. We need to look at our seasons like Jeremiah looked at his. Children, we don't want to seek salvation in our childhood, do we? Because in our childhood we want to have time to play with toys and have fun with games, and be childlike. And it's all right to play with dolls, and to play with Power Rangers, but don't forget Jesus. Jesus says in Mark 10:14: "Suffer the little children to come unto me, and forbid them not, for of such is the kingdom of heaven."

Youth, we don't want to seek salvation in our youth, do we? Because in our youth we are busy being preteens, and then we are busy being teenagers. It's all right for us to go to shows, and dance at the parties, and dress in style with style. But don't forget what Solomon says in Ecclesiastes 12:1: "Remember your Creator in the days of your youth, before the days of trouble come and the years approach when you will say, 'I find no pleasure in them.' "

Mature adults, we don't want to seek salvation in our maturity, do we? Young adults think they are too young, and older adults think they are too old. And most of us are too busy seeking to raise a family, or seeking to make some money, or seeking to survive. But Jesus said in Matthew 6:33, if you want to do anything, or if you want to be anything, or if you want to make anything out of your life: "Seek you first the kingdom of God and his righteousness, and all other things will be added unto you."

I want to ask this question. Children, is this the season to seek salvation? Youth, is this the season to seek salvation? Adults, is this the season to seek salvation? Old Folks, is this the season to seek salvation?

What happens if we don't have a season of salvation? What will happen to the abused child, if our children don't find salvation? What will happen to the motherless child, if our children don't find salvation? What will happen to the babe born out of wedlock, if our children don't seek salvation?

What will happen to our youth, if we don't have a season of salvation? What will happen in our schools, if our youth don't find salvation? What will happen in the neighborhood, what will happen in the "hood," if our youth don't seek salvation?

What will happen to our families, if fathers don't seek salvation? What will happen to our homes, if mothers don't seek salvation? Who is going to meet us in heaven, if our old folks don't seek salvation? Who is going to be left down in Hell, if we all don't seek salvation?

Is this the season to seek salvation? Maybe winter is too cold. Nobody wants to go to church in winter. Maybe spring is too wet. Too much rain, we need to stay inside. Maybe summer is too hot. And we have to enjoy ourselves sometime. Maybe the fall is too busy with baseball and football. Maybe, maybe ... The harvest is past, and summer is ended, and we are not saved.

The only place to seek salvation is here; the only time to seek salvation is now. So somewhere in the here and now, we need to seek salvation.

Lectionary Preaching
After Pentecost

The following index will aid the user of this book in matching the correct Sunday with the appropriate text during Pentecost. All texts in this book are from the series for Lesson One, Revised Common Lectionary. (Note that the ELCA division of Lutheranism is now following the Revised Common Lectionary.) The Lutheran and Roman Catholic designations indicate days comparable to Sundays on which Revised Common Lectionary Propers are used.

(Fixed dates do not pertain to Lutheran Lectionary)

Fixed Date Lectionaries *Revised Common (including ELCA)* *and Roman Catholic*	Lutheran Lectionary *Lutheran*
The Day of Pentecost	The Day of Pentecost
The Holy Trinity	The Holy Trinity
May 29-June 4 — Proper 4, Ordinary Time 9	Pentecost 2
June 5-11 — Proper 5, Ordinary Time 10	Pentecost 3
June 12-18 — Proper 6, Ordinary Time 11	Pentecost 4
June 19-25 — Proper 7, Ordinary Time 12	Pentecost 5
June 26-July 2 — Proper 8, Ordinary Time 13	Pentecost 6
July 3-9 — Proper 9, Ordinary Time 14	Pentecost 7
July 10-16 — Proper 10, Ordinary Time 15	Pentecost 8
July 17-23 — Proper 11, Ordinary Time 16	Pentecost 9
July 24-30 — Proper 12, Ordinary Time 17	Pentecost 10
July 31-Aug. 6 — Proper 13, Ordinary Time 18	Pentecost 11
Aug. 7-13 — Proper 14, Ordinary Time 19	Pentecost 12
Aug. 14-20 — Proper 15, Ordinary Time 20	Pentecost 13
Aug. 21-27 — Proper 16, Ordinary Time 21	Pentecost 14
Aug. 28-Sept. 3 — Proper 17, Ordinary Time 22	Pentecost 15
Sept. 4-10 — Proper 18, Ordinary Time 23	Pentecost 16
Sept. 11-17 — Proper 19, Ordinary Time 24	Pentecost 17

Sept. 18-24 — Proper 20, Ordinary Time 25	Pentecost 18
Sept. 25-Oct. 1 — Proper 21, Ordinary Time 26	Pentecost 19
Oct. 2-8 — Proper 22, Ordinary Time 27	Pentecost 20
Oct. 9-15 — Proper 23, Ordinary Time 28	Pentecost 21
Oct. 16-22 — Proper 24, Ordinary Time 29	Pentecost 22
Oct. 23-29 — Proper 25, Ordinary Time 30	Pentecost 23
Oct. 30-Nov. 5 — Proper 26, Ordinary Time 31	Pentecost 24
Nov. 6-12 — Proper 27, Ordinary Time 32	Pentecost 25
Nov. 13-19 — Proper 28, Ordinary Time 33	Pentecost 26
	Pentecost 27
Nov. 20-26 — Christ the King	Christ the King

Reformation Day (or last Sunday in October) is October 31 (Revised Common, Lutheran)

All Saints' Day (or first Sunday in November) is November 1 (Revised Common, Lutheran, Roman Catholic)

www.ingramcontent.com/pod-product-compliance
Lightning Source LLC
Chambersburg PA
CBHW071025040426
42443CB00007B/934